# THE NIGHT CHORUS

THE HUGH MACLENNAN POETRY SERIES

Editors: Allan Hepburn and Carolyn Smart

# The Night Chorus

## Harold Hoefle

McGill-Queen's University Press
Montreal & Kingston • London • Chicago

ISBN 978-0-7735-5492-4 (paper)
ISBN 978-0-7735-5591-4 (ePDF)
ISBN 978-0-7735-5592-1 (ePUB)

Legal deposit third quarter 2018
Bibliothèque nationale du Québec

Printed in Canada on acid-free paper that is 100% ancient forest free
(100% post-consumer recycled), processed chlorine free

Funded by the Government of Canada   Financé par le gouvernement du Canada      Canada Council for the Arts   Conseil des arts du Canada

We acknowledge the support of the Canada Council for the Arts,
which last year invested $153 million to bring the arts to
Canadians throughout the country.

Nous remercions le Conseil des arts du Canada de son soutien. L'an
dernier, le Conseil a investi 153 millions de dollars pour mettre de l'art
dans la vie des Canadiennes et des Canadiens de tout le pays.

**Library and Archives Canada Cataloguing in Publication**

Hoefle, Harold, 1959–, author
    The night chorus / Harold Hoefle.

    (The Hugh MacLennan poetry series)
    Poems.
    Issued in print and electronic formats.
    ISBN 978-0-7735-5492-4 (softcover). – ISBN 978-0-7735-5591-4 (ePDF).
    – ISBN 978-0-7735-5592-1 (ePUB)

    I. Title.  II. Series: Hugh MacLennan poetry series

    PS8565.O325N54 2018          C811'.6          C2018-903317-7
                                                   C2018-903318-5

This book was typeset by Marquis Interscript
in 9.5/13 New Baskerville.

*for Karen*

# CONTENTS

# THE NIGHT CHORUS

# A LOVING FOLLOW-THROUGH

At least it's not dripping off the kitchen table,
the wet cereal of my brain, but the front room's got
my Kyla and Jimbo, I hope not messy like me,
and *he's* already gone, he eff-ed right off,
the screen door banging at that orange moon,
and it was so him to do us after dark,
but that's my Brian, it's like I married
every nasty bit in the ten o'clock news.
Good that he called 911 (someone should mop),
though now for-sure he's barrelling out of town,
whipping along the ditch with a bottle in his crotch …
and isn't *cereal* a weird word? I am (was) serial,
as in serially attracted to the Brians,
the ones who chug whisky like beer,
who brag *I'll sleep when I'm dead* – those guys.
So there's me with my loser beacon, Yvonne told me,
blonde to blonde, party girl to party girl.
She opened and shut her fist in my face,
said *that's your forehead winking at crazies.*
Guess it's true, I could never get past men like him,
as if Brian were just the end product, exactly that,
but he's the one I chose, the one with the wooden bat,
taking down the world that tried to take him down,
and starting right at home with a big wind-up,
a smooth swing, and a loving follow-through.

# THE INSIDE DIRT

My father's focus was like water he tried
to cup. Age six, I saw the drip. On a hot day
he salved his itch, ditched his briefcase
by the lake and ran, wife and son in his wake.

Later … my mother prodding me with a dustpan
full of pebbles, crushed cups, balled-up chip bags,
all from my rusted Civic. Her scoff:
"Inside-dirt shows what you really are."

Glazed by morphine in her last bed,
she pulled my ear close and said,
"We're in a killing house,
the heads are in the buckets."

Now the absent father is back:
thin, bent, a bore.
I swim for hours in his talk.
I never touch the shore.

# DOWN THE ROADS

i

That Poff Road scofflaw is a florid Austrian
whose first spade hit granite, whose wife McGinty
bore three daughters she called his fates.
Back then he dealt in flint, for the girls were hard –
to keep still, to stop from asking questions.
Their mouths were always open:
pink, like chicks in a nest,
then lipsticked red, black, purple.
Voices would rise, fingers jab, cheeks flush,
*Daddy* the epithet they whipped him with.
If he went cold, silent, they knew what to do,
crowd him on the couch and lick his ears
until he cried and said *yes, anything, yes.*

On Wither Road a man's in full stride,
all Lennon glasses and leonine hair,
tied back or bandanna-ed, bouncing off his pack,
his plaid shirt untucked and he moves like 1972.
People say he was military, on leave, on furlough,
but went AWOL and now is going where –
and growing what – he can't when he holds a gun.

On Morest Road, Spence is running the combine at noon
with one arm in a sling and a bag of weed at his boots,
Leafs cap on his head, thoughts of keeping his line true
and getting his cast off – the doc said two weeks – so he can do
airy Sherry again (and again) in his car parked at the firebreak.
He's watching a hawk hover above a ditch and drop
straight down … nine hours on, Spence will look north and see
what he's been seeing all his life, a rolling back of pine forest,
hills swallowing the sun, and he's left with the silhouette
of a barn, a silo, a spire that needles the sky
and every dream of Spence Morest.

A postcard arrives from my sister
driving solo on a dawn highway,
cutting across the Mojave Desert.
She sketches the world of dun and ochre,
jonquil and terracotta, lizard-green and stone-grey.
Cacti and rattlers own the land.
She mentions a beer can
faded to silver, spiked on a stake.

On Crampton Road, a red fox is biting its back.
The man sticks his hand out the window,
the rushing air chills his palm, a balm in this heat.
He speeds along the ditch of bottles and snagged bags,
of burst milkweed fluff. A train screams.
He waits for rumble, for containers
to pass like rusted trailer-homes beside him,
and his new strapped-in girlfriend says
she can't forget the times her father
took her hand and said, *Come, walk with me.*

We drink at the big swim off Whiskey Bay Road,
its waters amber. Whispering *here's proof* to the county judge,
we nudge him with a forty-pounder of Canadian Club.
He flaps his hands and shouts *No! No! No!*
We laugh.

Patched and potholed: that's Melgund Road,
neglected by crews paid to lavish tar and roller love
on the Trans Canada,
but you might catch a bass in the biggest hole,
kids swim in it. Forget the pink lupin in the ditch,
the weeds and daisies; forget, too, the circle of rushes
that tilt your way from the edge of Sester's pond.
Sester: he's eaten fries every day since he was twelve,
and when he's drunk he likes to take potshots
at crows, grouse, wood pheasants, turkey vultures
and cars driven by strangers – he's got a blind for that.

On Magpie River Road the talk should flow – but doesn't.
The hitchhiker calls the morning *pretty damp, eh?*
but won't look your way, though he wags a knobby finger
at the white cross stuck in roadside dirt and mutters,
*my brother after too many*, then stares at racing telephone poles,
creosote-black and half-buried, each top another cross.
The hitchhiker shows you blue-red eyes and asks in a low voice,
with slow words, if you'll buy him a draft at the Legion,
says he'll owe you, and nods before adding
he never welshes, never has and never will.

Lochwinnoch Road. Not the *Gaeltacht* anymore,
no arm-of-the-sea to be seen,
no winnowing of chaff or minnows,
instead a tawny deer and fawns all stilled by your stare,
a cardinal flower flaming its riverbank petals,
and your mother a woman who cannot forget
the one smile she never returned, when she was twenty,
when she read books, when she had hope.

On Schiefelbein or Schlick, and Waldhof of course,
on rocky land that we made ours,
nobody crows *The past is always with us*,
but no one has forgotten pride, it doubles us over
in dark beneath the pointing stars, the farmwork done,
our heads all cicada buzz and the loud tick-down
of computerized machinery only our sons can fix –
though snarkily, snorting – these sons who pay tuition
for their brand-loving kids in the gridlock city of Mammon,
where people stare at the concrete they walk on …
Listen: on these roads, grey hair and wrinkles
get respect: suspenders beat disbelief. Ha!
Yes, we love our loden jackets, and our Tyrolean hats
sport feathers plucked from the pheasants we shot.
But go ahead, mock: *faux Arcadian, pseudo sylvan,*
*rustic rabble* … as the sheep say: *Behhh!*
You and your culture: we hear the word, we grab our hammers.
No, here's what matters: Sunday church.
We're first for the first service; we end with song, triumphant.
Then we haul in pots of plum dumplings and still-warm soup.
The tables are long, wall to basement wall, planed in our barns.
Just look: we're brushed, ironed, polished; backs straight;
faces shaved or made-up, all reserved for one another.
Poised. But … I'll hush my voice … come visit. Please. Now.
Drive down our roads, post your photos
of deep-green fields, turquoise barns and shining silos.
Post a hundred, a thousand, ten thousand or more.
Our children want us gone.

# CAMPING AT LAC LA PÊCHE

The stories were pretty good,
told by lit figures in the dark:
N's friend, who knows the Bordeaux guards
by their first names and, last month,
got his face slapped in a bar;
R's sister, who shot an air gun at a party
and hit his leg; R the same night,
watching a buddy bend down
and French-kiss his German shepherd.
M just laughed; M, the pathologist
who grades tumours, reviews autopsies.

Dawn. A dragonfly cuts triangles out of air,
and men are casting lures in arcs
that catch the light, flash the brightness.
High, child voices bounce across the lake.
Rushes flutter, green against blue,
and a loon offers a long tremolo.
A Cesna drones the bass line for this sudden song.

I set down my mug
and step to the water,
sandals slapping granite.
Wind arches the pines,
but a triangle of air
is still there, in my head,
a bell that clangs one thought.
Intensify.

Scrum and huddle and corner kick,
set the pick and pick the corner,
drop-pass and behind-the-back,
go wide, go inside, kick the last quarter,
sit in the slot, block the shot, control the T,
roll right and drive the baseline,
hip check, poke check, finish our checks –
but still we're losing –
so we play the body, the trap, the wall,
we jab, slash, and elbow the head
until we're only down by five,
then I try my kill shot
to keep our hopes alive.

# CHARADE

What if Caesar wanted to die?
The knives easing into flesh
asking to be honeycombed,
the blood a spreading salve
for the sickness of worry.

What if Odysseus hated travel?
His fantasy the home fires,
the harpist who sang of someone else's fight
with siren and giant; with Cyclops and Poseidon.
What if *the crafty man* only wanted
Penelope's touch and the sight of his son
pulling up rocks, planting seed?

And what if, in all the years of exile,
Ovid was happy in Tomis?
Imagine his stance by the Black Sea,
and how its lapping waters consoled,
told him the endless wrenching of his Rome-sick heart
was only natural. Perhaps the sea taught the poet:
the sublime was not a change of form, but the repetition of.

Fired by dreams and whimsy, I want
other versions: Juliet bored by Romeo's fawning;
Virgil asking Dante to take him by the hand;
and, on stage, Othello admitting his adventures
to the open-armed, forgiving Desdemona,
who cannot stop his suicide.

And what if my deepest love,
my pact with the evening kiss,
the wish to hold and listen,
the hand reaching for hand –
what if all my loving hours
are mere charade,
the flapping of my heart's flag
because I fear the quiet.

# AIR

A rushing scream
slams the stalks
into a death-field,
near the watching rocks.

No wind is ruled.
So why shout or sing?
Why spin the windmills?
Why anything?

Mystery's her dress of tulle;
coat and cap; flying frills.
Delight is whipping loose,
the toss and fight!

Stillness
she cannot choose.
Like the rain,
she's got to move.

That's not despair.
A wind is never held.
The hand, the reaching branch
gets all there is.

# AMSTERDAM

A napkin sketch, done by the old man
whose name in Dutch was duck hunter.
To show me how the kill works, he drew
a circle fringed by stars: pond, hunters.
Near the artist stood the barman, all paunch,
slitting the froth off a glass stamped
with a black triple X, the city symbol.

But the old man's talk … he paused once
and brought his face to mine, his capillaries
the finest red web. "Killing thrills" –
his whisper when I glanced towards
the corner, the stuffed orangutan there,
mouth open, black eyes wide and staring back.

# IN THE BATACLAN

Above him is rasping
through a mask.
Shoes *tack-tack* across
the beer-spill floor
he's pressed against.
His heart, the only beat he knows.

Here, just minutes before,
guitars and heat, lights and cheers,
the crush-hug of a thousand others.

He risks a glimpse from one slit eye.

The room's gone prone.
Then nearing steps,
a whistling through teeth.
He shuts his eye but still sees
the red glow of exit signs.

A sudden A K burst
like a popcorn maker –
a man aims at sound, movement.
The smell of smoke blends
with beer and gunpowder.

People will talk,
the candles and stories
flickering in the fates
of the murdered, the murderer.
Or the other words:
martyr, hero, victim.

His killer wears a wired belt.
Here, at the summit of their lives,
the shared chill of drying sweat.

## WORLDS

I sit on the backseat of the stopped bus and watch
a girl's head drift onto the shoulder of a lady
with a square bag at her feet, I hear teen boys
in sweatpants talk of pussy and calculus,
I smell the gel coating the head of the guy
listening to Beck on his iPod, I feel the pointy elbow
of a woman on my left who's got her head bent into
*The Man Without Qualities*, I catch the joy of girls
negotiating who'll skip class and who'll take notes,
I laugh at the sudden bounce of a ball as a boy dribbles
on the floor while staring down an old man's frown,
and when the bus jolts forward I'm surprised by your whisper
in my ear of how you've sat placidly on my right
and watched me watch others, of how in your homeland
no one does that anymore, of how last summer
a man with a necklace of children's fingers walked past you
and that same day someone said a Muslim had been crucified
on a church door, your whisper followed by a nudge
that makes me turn to confront your face and watch you
roll up a blouse-sleeve to show me tiny black eyes,
the cigarette burns you say decided your – this – exile.

# ICE FIRES

A lattice of shadows lies on the snow road
like the black veins of birch in moonlight,
as if the forest is revealing what's unseen,
like a secret being told of secret beings.

We cross patches of ice, our steps measured.
Somewhere close, deer huddle in a yard,
ears lifting at the scratch of our shuffle.
The moon is a fingernail; the hunter's belt slung low.
Earlier, we heard ice crack in the bay,
the shore a home to jumbles
of chunks and slabs, like fire pits of ice.

When the snow gods leave the forest
and hunch over an ice fire –
the blue-white glow of ice wood –
its heat will warm the gods
who pity us, the proudly intrepid,
moving down a frozen road in darkness,
far from all the fuss of lights,
two more beings who think themselves free.

# NIGHT GHAZALS

i

Hot August, and in the bar a woman with legs
of coffee-coloured marble
wants to know what's up. I'm looking down.

Almost funny, what he told her at the last table.
How, in the dark, she looks like his mother.

The barman said his biggest mistake was quitting school
in grade eight. He flipped his grey ponytail,
told me he should've quit in grade six.

Zigzagging moral compass, innumerable black pints,
someone's stories of cocaine,
a tall girl who wrote your number on her arm:

bar nights are like eye colour, like friends:
do you want to change them?

In April a blind girl in Graz stood on a step,
talked of hating ice cream. The sun glared.
Smiling, she asked what I do in the afternoon.

Austria. An uncle hanged himself, a cousin walked
into a speeding truck. It's good luck to see a chimney sweep.

An art-show poster in Vienna: with one hand a naked woman
points a gun at her head; with the other, she points one at me.

He says he does heroin because he's got to. He paints walls
all day, looks away and sees drop sheets, smeared cans.
White paint. Always. White. Paint.

Night … the demanding clang and cadence
of a passenger train.
Straps hang from the overhead rack. Hang and swing.

Books brim the sidewalk recycling box, from Cheever's
*Stories* to *You're So Lonely When You're Dead.*

Spread on the road is a creosote lake. Nothing
is getting done: so flit your eyes.

The homeless boy coughs, says the cops keep
trying to throw him out of outside.

A horn tears the night air; noise mocks her subjects. You want
the passing trains to whisper before you go off the rails.

Yes, heroin and Louis, my East Van friend, his dog
licking his basement face: not lonely, just dead.

The grilling sun, one lane on one bridge open
and the flagman's sign is STOP. More than exhaust fumes.

But down the sidewalk strides our Helen:
high heels, dark glasses: fuck me, fuck you.

The bare-chested boy and girl stand in the painting
*Discretion*, her hand over his mouth.

After dark, outside the Fez train station, the fat procuress
points at the curvy girl, then my crotch.

                             I enter a bar,
bouncers at the door. One's hand is bandaged, one's arm
is in a sling. When I nod good night, they touch their hearts.

## WHAT FALLS

Soap in the shower,
the towel off the rack,
the shirt the hanger,
the jacket the peg.

Coffee drips,
papers fly;
books tip,
pens dive.

The ice cubes drop
and mix with dust,
a grass rake slips
from garage nail.

Last night a star
left its contrail,
a sparkle
that failed.

Grief falls
like hair
across
a face.

# STRONG TEA

The day you came back,
a leak had pouched the ceiling,
a grey drywall saucer
with a hole in the middle.
But you and I,
we drank strong tea
and talked,
the ping-pong
of word and window glance,
of fast laugh and topic switch.

After a look outside,
you said the capped waves
were angry.
And when you left
you didn't wave,
capping off
not just your thought.

I waved at your back,
my hand flopping,
as if the wrist were broken.

# DRIFTING

Mist is circling the lake,
a first-light dance
the sun won't see
but knows is there
and wants to burn.

The shore at dusk,
silhouettes bursting
like fireworks: gulls.
Screaming, they rise,
weave, dip and drift.

The geese are higher,
hundreds of black letters
printing the violet page,
a scrawl of language
between the margins of land and sky.

Darkness: a heavy stone.
I miss the snows
that gusted, paused,
gusted across the lake
like the ghosts of fathers gone.

# ENGLAND

### i

The laughter of locals and tourists
jostling at the winter solstice.
Tonight's parade will move from street to strand,
with paper-and-willow lanterns held high
and offered to bonfires, shadows of flame
crossing open mouths, smoke curling moonward.
It's "Burning the Clocks" in Brighton; the music's live.

Evening sky is still milky blue.
Plodding in sand beyond the Pier,
my soldier-friend talks of Syria,
of barrel bombs – his hand mimes
a chopper's flight – or the other custom
where the Air Force scores a junky car.
Clamp, climb, drop.

We pass a bronze statue of a runner,
arms straight up.
I scan the Channel's dark waters,
the sunset stretch of plum-and-orange light,
the colour of bruises. Perhaps of shouts.
Panic shouts. Unlike those I hear now
and turn to follow, crossing the soft, cool sand.

The British Museum, stone battles of centaur and Lapith,
then the pub, bulky Jonners with his need to confess:
"I love my son, I really do, but sometimes he's slightly shit."
Soon Jonners was blathering about oil-and-gas
and how he's drilled in sixty-six countries, a number
I knew he stole from the betting poster above my head.
Still, Jonners kept on bringing beer, tall pints of an ale
called *Doom* – I took that seriously, along with Jonners' eyes,
like dark holes, like ancient caves in the land of hedgerows,
beyond which lie the black sacks of hay, baled
in fields that also reach their own horizons.

A mud towpath, and every brickwork bridge
an eyebrow arched at my approach.
Along the canal, puddles mark
this trail like a spotted snake,
or the hundred eyes of that mythic guardian
whose name I never remember.
I jog on, splashing past a houseboat
with drawn curtains, past mallards
and circling moorhens. A magpie swoops,
a swan hisses, its neck hooked like an umbrella's.
Now the mud-squelch of someone on foot.
His hoodie's up, his grimace averted.
I glance away – looking means interest
in the naked show of pain.

# SOME GUY

blew the stop
ran the red
cut me off
threw a beer
and said I'm dead.

Some guy was here,
calling me Sweetie.
He touched my knee,
took my shoes
and found the booze.

Some guy played the clown,
a painted sack
all slumpy-spent.
He read this and said
I'm not what you meant.

# SLIDING GLASS

The door opened with a groan,
the remote buttons-down on the couch
where blankets hid the lie I thought
had died there, in their arms.
She caught me looking at plastic, presswood: the cheap goods
she said never cheated the room of real love.

Her hand reached, came near, withdrew –
as if another touch were ruin.
Outside her building, a truck's ramp was lowered,
the rollers shining like rows of silver teeth.
Her laugh echoed; I kept watch from above.
The load came in crates.

A woman used a pushcart to wheel them down
the walk. A breeze tried to steal her scarf.
She scanned the balconies, one hand against the sun.

Hard knocks, my walk to the door,
and behind me the sound of sliding glass,
of wind that slit the curtain like a dress
and wafted another laugh. The last.

# IN THE NAME OF THE FATHER

"Tim Davis! Still alive! You ponytailed old hippie,
you're not worms yet! And speaking of, I used the ones
I got from watering my yard and caught a nice pike yesterday,
just past the trestle bridge, you know, where we swam
in grade ten when Donnie did that stupid thing,
his poor mother – and how's yours doing? I love Betty,
she always put an Oreo in my hand when I ran
into your kitchen, and even after I did time,
my biceps covered in naked women, she'd see me
and say, 'Take a cookie, Alfie.' My mom? On assisted-
living, down by Grimsby – but hey, Timmie, sorry 'bout
your old man, Sam told me – what, a year ago?
That guy who made a left on a red? Fucker!
I heard he got off, too … let's learn where he lives
and make him pay – I know all the tricks.
Let's do it: your dad was good people.
You got piggyback rides past my house,
you'd wave your cowboy hat with that big sweeping motion,
one arm 'round his neck like reins,
but the only problem was, and the thing is,
you taught me envy – remember,
when my dad heard I came home in a cop car
for stealing hockey cards, then no more Mr Nice Guy –
nope, it was Tomato Face bouncing me off the walls
with me pissing myself the whole time and Mom sayin'
'You're hurting him, Gerald.' Anyways,
everyone talks about love and hate – how 'bout fear?
But don't worry, Timmie, I won't wuss out on you,
I'll do that guy who killed your dad, you watch,
I'll make his face look like pizza – "

# UNDERFOOT

A week of burnt things, hot air.
Whatever could, stuck to something else.
We sweated up the walk to see
the man you could not avoid: Gerry,
the janitor and rent collector.

Sun-glare in the foyer
and a potted Jerusalem rose.
Across the road, the lilacs hung.
A kayaker was twirling through
the haze of Valois Bay.
You pressed a button and shut your eyes.

In your fingers: twelve damp cheques
for the first floor of that crooked house
between bay and highway.

Things did go wrong: fuses blew,
pipes burst, the heating collapsed.
A door would slam and he'd be there,
grunting through your rooms,
splintering his words: *'kay, 'get it.*
Your daughter hid,
her fingers texting dismay.

But Gerry hung around, got underfoot.
Often, he stood in your kitchen –
a wrench in one hand, cigarette in the other –
or he slouched against the sink,
arms along the counter,
his pose a mock crucifixion.

Two packs a day – anyone could tell.
His skin parchment-yellow,
his cough like rocks rattled in a bag.
Still, Gerry could've been seventy or sixty:
the wiry body, the full head of grey hair,
the mojo born of who knew what.
And though he grunted, though paint
clotted his eyebrows, he'd notice
every torn screen or sagging hinge,
the linoleum curling in all your corners.

But our visit: we buzzed
his place; we buzzed again.

entwines a birch,
a puzzling blood sash –
why this birch, in this forest
of old- and second-growth,
a realm of autumn cool,
with – if I stop – a quiet
only disturbed by bounding squirrels,
a fluttering grouse.

The ribbon's the one human sign
where the past is millennia
of hunters, woodsmen,
travellers – and I
am someone else who walks
amid the wooded spires,
the cones-and-needles understorey,
the birdsong of claim, courtship, and warning.

## A CALLER
*(after Zbigniew Herbert)*

All of it's been good,
what's next will be good,
and what's up now
is not bad.

In a nest of skin and sinew
there lived a bird
whose wings beat near the heart.
We called it *stress*, or *love*.

At dusk we hooked fingers
and stood by the rushing Sadness River.
It showed us ourselves, the lie in the eye,
and asked what we admit to.

Look,
the calling bird has dropped
as if shot;
the river is sunk in sand.

Naïve like kids,
calloused like seniors,
we are free,
full of choice, good to go.

Tonight a voice at the door,
a smiling man with a bottle.
I lean into his face:
"Who are you?"

"The students of Classics say *Seneca*"
– his breath was hot –
"but those who have no Latin
call me *Death*."

# CASTLES

Standing eye-deep in a sunset river,
you stare at pinks, mauves, greens
that spread from you to the cedar shore
where the deer see you, the sandpipers do not care,
and osprey wish you were a fish.

You want to stay in the moment,
thankful the day has loosened her grip
on the heat-tarp she threw down
and pulled tight over your life.

Before dark, there's time to mull,
and the river mellows you.
You watch a tern skim the water.
The far hills sleep like huddled giants,
and worry seems further than either shore.

Except for the moon's razor glints,
the river's gone shale-grey,
cooling your skin,
though one thought tugs
like the current itself:

your doubt has lit the kindling
of a future you stoke until
it flickers and licks at the dark air,
a flame to nurture here, near the sand
where your children build their own castles.

# PARK EX

The grinding whine of a cargo train.
A day of grey cirrus and a little blue,
a parlour in Park Ex, the dark-suited men
with their soft vowels that rise, descend,
the tall mothers who grip the children
and at the hall's far end, a young man dead.

Blue-eyed wild in school, when he laughed
his forelock danced; dodging questions,
his eyebrow flew up and stayed up.
Sure, he sucked oxygen from the room,
but all his antics gave us back our breath:
we who gaped, whether we stood or sat.

A man with grey hair and a ragged side-part
has the same eyes, but sunken. Bagged.
We avoid the hallway's row of guests;
a ceremony starts. The man cannot talk –
or look at the casket, the white face with
the mouth curled upward, sharing the joke.

# THE COAST

Turn after hairpin turn,
the plunging cliff, the rising road.
He wondered: why drive into air
just to visit her asthmatic aunt?

The girl stared at sun-glints
stretching to where sea met sky.
"Mine's the blues," she muttered,
before the car skidded to the edge.

His eyes fixed on a vulture,
its brown head buried
in a dog's stomach.
The head bobbed.

She wanted the boy
to comfort her with a touch,
but he drove at the bird until it flew off,
tilting towards the burnt hills.

Tight descent; the boy braked his way down,
and at sea-level said his first words
in two white-knuckle hours.
"The dead eating the dead."

The girl blew the bangs
off her forehead.
"Matt, that is so you:
it sounds good, and means *nada*."

He did not look over,
he just eyed an oncoming truck
and wondered why it had to be brown,
and why his life felt so wrong.

## PASSING BY WITH TWO GUYS AT MIDNIGHT, A GIRL TELLS HER FRIEND

Just pop your earbuds in
and lie the fuck down,
that's all you need.

… like Sally Mander, her life mangled from Day One,
but what a move last June in Normandy, book-in-hand
and sunning on someone's mansion roof,
she had the radio on loud when her parents found her
and shouted, "You belly-pierced gutter slut!"
Well, Sally chose to woman up. After shifting the sneers
to a man selling mangoes in the cobbled street,
she shoved her folks right off the roof. It's true.
That night she got a flight via Paris to Manhattan,
became a dresser of mannequins and loved a man
on remand. I asked why – in the dockside
Mandala Café – and Sally blinked, told me the romance
felt mandated, as if the fates (her supposed long-haired sisters)
decreed that felon fell for felon. While she spoke,
the first chords of Sinéad's "Mandinka" came blasting
from the speakers. My feet twitching, I leaned forward
to gaze into the black eyes of Sally Mander,
and when I asked if she had a code, a mantra she followed,
her eyes slit, her mouth went small, her skin
translucent, she slithered off towards the river –
a move, a last note I could never manage,
strumming on the strings of my mandolin.

# CROSSING

A bag of bread and milk in hand,
I stood staring into a whorl,
a mesh of wet branches
silhouetted by a streetlamp,
a great orb of shining drops,
a dark and perfect space
that fixed me to the sidewalk
and loosed my thoughts,
as if an after-rain portal
could prompt pedestrian
images, like the one
of a toy, peach-yellow,
buried in snow by the crossing
at Emerson, into Canada.

The girls get on the bus like ducks,
a waggle of shorts-and-T-shirt skinnies,
tall to small. One has egg-shaped glasses;
another, flushed cheeks; the last walks
like a queen in flip-flops. Do the hurts
get feathered over in the gaggle? And if
a bad dream lingers, will the light scorching
through windows burn it off, just as the clothes-toss
bedroom-mess is forgotten?
*Jolt. Lurch.* Bodies stagger.
The girls keep their balance,
keep whispering, stay on their phones.
Glasses Girl is smoothing Flip-Flops' hair –
I go back to my book. I cannot find the line.
In the history of abortion, three are mine.

# DOWNTOWN

The city was painted toenails
and sweat dripping from chins.
Verdigris coloured the college spires;
poplars fought the wind, their leaves bristling.

Someone I could not see
pulled a rope of children
across the school lawn.
One day, some would come back,
the others fanning out into travel,
trades, screen- and face-jobs;
into mortgage- and rent-ville; into pills,
guilty hookups, bad roommates,
and bosses easy to fear, easy to hate.

Outside an office tower,
a woman tapped off her ashes.
"The worst is dreaming about work,
then you wake up and go there."

## MY LAST BADASS

A skeleton danced on his hoodie.
Skull rings barnacled his left hand.
Plus the beard – the clots of hair –
and the leg tattoo, a death match
of helmets, knives, blood-drip.

Sniffling in the crowded clinic,
I thought about family, its sinkhole –
was *this* badass born into hate?
Maybe he taught the kids with Special Needs,
tween boys and girls pressing their heads
into his chest when he stood near.
Or looks were truth: he was mean.
Shades of *Clockwork Orange*,
like telling old ladies on the bus
to *fuck off* when they gazed at his seat.
Still … the deft left hand,
whipping out his phone
to check his Facebook feed …
was he a normal-ass?
Though the rings belonged,
and the camouflage scarf
that hung from his black shorts,
from the ass of Badass.

I sat close, diagonal, waiting
to hear my number called.

Badass scratched his beard.

Now I knew! Screamo-band guitarist!
The white gauze, wrapped around
his right hand – busted on-stage
in a rage (possibly mock),
and *not* from punching someone
in the face, someone who stared,
who took notes, whose nose
was already broken.

A cough turned my head.
Badass chose that moment
to reach over, clamp his good hand
on my knee and level his eyes at mine.
He said his kind were always stared at
by guys like me – *geek macho-envy*,
he called it, his wink hovering
between pity and threat
before he plucked the notepad
from my hands, tore out the pages
and stuffed them in his mouth.
A black-shirt guard approached,
but Badass did his lockdown glare
while he chewed and chewed,
bulging his cheeks before he spat.
The goo splattered my face,
far softer than a punch
and done for the one he had to impress.
Because a badass needs someone
to be badder than, like my old need
to be more good. But I stood,
I rolled my shoulders,
shook out my arms,
and he also rose,

his hands hanging down,
fingers flexing,
and for the first time
I moved in,
I stepped up,
at last
I would be bad.

## BRIDGES

High sun, mid-river, a spider swung
on a wisp and hit the water,
surprising you in the bow
and twinning in my head
with a different drop,
the friend who jumped off the Cartier
as if he'd become his own worst card
and tossed it in
to finish and go home.

While I watched the spider float,
I asked about your mint garden,
how you press your face
into the leaves to de-stress.

You stuck out the paddle
and gave the spider a raft.
You were like that.

# DEATH OF A POET

*(i.m. Judith Ariana Fitzgerald, 1952–2015)*

Your life was lightning. You struck a room,
flushed and flamed every cheek, then turned away
from the burning stumps of all who wanted you,
smoke curling like your hair in summer.

\*

Childhood: yours was not green buds, soft air.
Hunger tore at you and your siblings; the mother
never there. So you scavenged alleys: the bins,
the cans. Fear and weakness fed on you.

\*

Your poems, the postcard rooms you lived in,
the angles of a minute-by-minute existence
jutting out and in: your life was Cubist.
One edge was a writer's yard,
the deck of that lakeside A-frame where,
below the maples, the poets heard
you read and made comments, shared laughs,
but mostly stared – *gamine, sylph, sibyl?*
Like others, the poets wanted more:
the thighs you crossed, the hair you tossed.
The winning moves you learned from loss.

\*

The crack of a bat was something
you also knew. In bars, at parties,
your tongue could sever anyone, but when
church bells tolled at twilight – off you'd run
to be alone, to stand in shadow.

*

At a Windsor desk, your lookout on the slow river,
you'd watch boats pass and water ride the shore.
You thought of people you knew, or had known:
that carousel of friend/contact/met-once/ex-something.
One memory remained: the man you loved the most,
whose torment kept his own hands at his throat.

*

It's after two on a dull, December day.
But you'd be right at home with these muted tones
of cat-grey, ochre; of wet snow dripping down
the brick. Still, you had to paint the vision
in your head – blue shot through with black –
a backdrop for your own red hair and white skin.
Your only prayer: that art let you let go.

# THE DIVER

As if she'll form a circle,
she lifts her arms
but stops when
her body's a perfect T
at the dock's end,
then her fingers curve upward
into the cold September air,
and her shoulders pump once
to shuck whatever clings,
for something always does,
memory a closet of clothes
that hang from bent wire,
the clothes you never chose
or cannot find.

# PLAYING DEAD AMONG THE DEAD

Our skin is splotched. We hobble down the hall of pink tile,
the mall concourse, where lighting turns sallow the few
who aren't. But our walkers help us avoid a fall, and the mall
has ramps, railings, benches, all set up to fend off exhaustion,
though the air is rank with missed chances, as if Chance itself
has rotted. And so the throat constricts, the sphincter wants
to shut, or has shut, just watch our shuffle, table legs move
faster, but damn the painters of this place, they chose white
to defeat us, its shout of clean, fresh, alive, while these shops
cater to decrepits, polyester rules on sales' racks,
though staring for too long hurts our necks. And Hope left
years ago, we were sometimes happy, smiling at a stranger
was what we did, and today the stranger's a terrorist
and everything's for sale, including us, the sneered-at seniors,
the ones who fought abroad, who moaned *Momma* in the dark
on that rocky beach, after playing dead among the dead
till deep night. We know about depth, and talking too much,
we don't have to, we're your future, our crutches
your *memento mori*, we of the long or gone memory,
each of us a bag of bones some god could use for soup.
Still, no need to hate us, our stoop and stupor, we hate it more,
what we see when we unbutton, the folds, the purple,
and when our clothes hit the floor, they no longer get twisted
with someone else's, and even if Paris was yesterday,
Paris is forgotten. And here's the pharmacy! The best,
the biggest store, with wide aisles and perfume waft, pastel walls
and calming music, the smiling staff who always wait for us,
and the turnstiles gleam silver, but only turn one way.

# ROSIE

I still see a tablecloth checked red-and-white,
and how a bottle stood before I sat.
With her, my father's sister, I once made
my claim to youth: I'd walk across her land,
sleeping in fields until Vienna.
The skin crinkled 'round my aunt's eyes.
More beer. I never asked a thing.

This blonde and grey-eyed woman,
her fingers combing a prisoner's hair
in a barn, a field, a hidden somewhere
in that wartime summer. Her past and his
made the world a present, but their son
became a summons from the Occupier,
the black steel helmets. Love was done.

They say her fingers raked her face,
the lines of blood condemning
the blue betrayer eyes of her father,
who waved his hands
and showed his palms.
Her cheeks became her speech:
she'd never enter his house again.

\*

Now her hands unwind the gauze.
She guides my touch to her foot,
the open sore a nurse will bandage.
I look past my aunt to the vase
of bluebells – the droop of small helmets –
then I settle my eyes on hers, their grey,
her best and last defence.

# DOWN THE ROADS (REPRISE)

We're serious here, all furrowed fields and eyebrows.
Disquiet? No, a shared coldness, with death our neighbour,
accidents our uncles, police warrants our prodigal sons;
with homes built of wood we milled and stone we quarried;
with guns our birthright. Our first love is a thrown punch.
Here, *sorry* is never heard; pity's a prompt for fists.
A man who can't lift his weight is gone – driven off.
On Maggrah Road we live and die. We tell ourselves
that in a world ruined by soft hands, fate has kissed us.

The swallows swoop at you on Moate Road,
feinting at the windshield, so just imagine
the happy chatter when you curse –
or, even better, lose control of the wheel.
Distractions include the field of bright yellow,
fenced in barbed wire, post to post.
Someone's woven a vine between two strands,
a trellis, red-flowered, and you've no idea why
or what it means, as if everything had a meaning,
as if believing that will let you walk
on solid ground and have a chance at love,
or knowing why you don't.

They say the funny people live on Seldom Seen,
their lives a daily trade in stale jokes and new ways
of finding ghosts, the shades of family both long
and lately dead, clothes comically dated –
collars flop, skirts drag – yet their airy selves
a balm, a comfort to the living persons there,
unlike the school-bus driver's grin. She's new, but
her seats are torn, her brakes in bad need of repair.

North Road takes you, the blacktop curving round boreal lakes,
past red and white and jack pine, past rock cuts and clouds
of knowing flies, past tilted erratics and fallen trailers,
past a scarecrow in your father's shirt. The windshield
is whipped by willows, your thoughts by a memory,
the time a friend called in need – you drive on,
your stare defied by the dropping sun, still too bright to watch.

At kitchen tables along Black Dog Road,
the chins get propped in hands, prescriptions shared
by friends, their ears filled with the hollow clicks
and echoes of jiggled pills, spread out for checkers.
Here, waking up means looking down to face the dog.
Its tooth is long and unforgiving.

A touch away, the rain's *pock-pock-pock*
resounds in this windowed box speeding through green
the downpour blurs and deepens.
The road climbs, dips, arcs, cupping the world in a curve.
The radio sputters another love song.
Far above, treetop-high, two crows eye the dull shine
of moving metal. I slow, click the music off
and slide past a skeletal barn, grey slats on a grass hill.
I brake in gravel, the rain still drilling the roof
like a father telling a son the same thing, over and over.
But the rain weakens; a stretch of mist hangs in a field;
cawing stops. A turkey vulture completes a turn
and drops from sight, replaced by an image
from the last town, from a driveway's lip,
a dresser spilling clothes and at its foot
a wooden sign, the letters slashed in red: *Take Me*

# NOTES

### "Down the Roads"

*The past is always us*: this phrase appears in the sequence's tenth poem. The words belong to Bengali poet Rabindranath Tagore (1861–1941). The complete sentence reads: "The past is always with us, for nothing that once was time can ever depart."

### "In the Bataclan"

This poem is set in the Parisian club where a terrorist attack occurred on the concert night of November 13, 2015. Three gunmen entered the venue and killed eighty-nine people.

### "Rosie"

This poem commemorates the life of Maria Rosa "Rosie" Gasser (1922–2012), of Kennelbach, Austria.

## DEDICATIONS

"Camping at Lac La Pêche" is for James Dixon.
"*Homo ludens*" is for Alexander MacLeod.
"England" is for Vinay Talwar and David York.
"In Transit" is for MCP.
"The Diver" is for Marie Legault.

# ACKNOWLEDGMENTS

Thanks to the editors of the following journals, in which some of the poems first appeared in their present or previous forms: *Grain, Matrix, Prairie Fire, Scrivener, The Antigonish Review, The Dalhousie Review, The Malahat Review, The Missing Slate, The Moth (Ireland), The Windsor Review,* and *vallum.*

"Down the Roads" won the Great Blue Heron Poetry Award (2014), sponsored by *The Antigonish Review.* "A Loving Follow-Through" won the Banff Centre Bliss Carman Award (2014), sponsored by *Prairie Fire*; the poem also won a silver medal at the National Magazine Awards (2016), and was featured in "Feral City" (2015), a collaborative exhibit of artist and writers' work at the Undercurrent Projects Gallery in New York. The poem was twinned with a painting by Toronto artist Misha Lobo.

Thanks to the friends who helped me shape some of these poems, or helped in other ways: Kevin Bushell, Andrew Cash, Misha Lobo, Alexander MacLeod, Olivia Raco, Richard Simas, and Elisha Wagman. For full-on manuscript comments, thanks to Douglas Brown, Simon Fanning, and David O'Meara. Thanks to my family for ongoing support: Karen Rhodes (my first reader), Daniel and Kirsten. My gratitude, also, goes to the team at MQUP, especially Mark Abley and Allan Hepburn. Final thanks to Geoffrey Cook – for years of poem comments; for help with organizing the manuscript; for counsel.